MACHIAVELLI AND THE ELIZABETHANS

By Dr. MARIO PRAZ

Read March 21, 1928

THE popular legend of Machiavelli, the wicked politician, originated in France, as is well known, at the
time of Catherine de' Medici: it represented the culmi-
nation of that anti-Italian feeling which naturally spread
among French people under the rule of the Florentine sovereign. The preferments given to the Italian adventurers
who crowded the French Court, the policy of the Crown
in religious matters, were mainly if not solely responsible
for the unprecedented amount of obloquy cast on the name
of the Florentine Secretary. Upon Machiavelli's head were
visited all the abuses committed by the Italian favourites,
chiefly their rapacity, which rankled above all in the hearts
of the French. It is only too natural that partiality to
foreigners on the part of a sovereign should arouse resent-
ment in a country. It has always been so, in all times and
lands. Odium was attached to the Catalan knights in the
service of the Neapolitan king, Robert of Anjou ('l' avara
povertà di Catalogna'—*Parad.* viii), and to the Dutch
followers of William III of Orange, no less than to the
Florentine courtiers of Catherine de' Medici. The position
of these latter was rendered still more odious by the religious factor. The several grounds of national and religious
hatred against the Italians in France can be well studied in
a curious pamphlet written in English soon after the acces-
sion of Henry IV of France, possibly by a French huguenot.
There we find that the anti-Italian feeling, in its final stage,
has blossomed into a seemingly scientific theory. The title
runs: *A Discovery of the great subtiltie and wonderfulwisedomeof the
Italians, whereby they beare sway over the most part of Christendome,*

and cunninglie behave themselves to fetch the Quintescence out of the peoples purses: Discoursing at large the meanes, howe they prosecute and continue the same: and last of all, convenient remedies to prevent all their pollicies herein.[1] The author draws from the first a distinction between the Septentrional and Occidental peoples and the Meridional nations: all the advantages possessed by the latter, chiefly as regards statecraft, are traced to the subtlety of the air.[2] The former, on the other hand, are described as labouring under 'a grosse humour ingendred in them, by reason of the grosnes and coldnes of the aier'. In the persons of Romulus and Numa Pompilius the writer sees prefigured two kinds of government among the Italians: Romulus founded his state on murder, Numa was a 'most subtill and ingenious inventor of a forged religion, to establish his owne government'. 'God would manifest unto us, that this nation should serve itselfe heereafter, with murthers and apparence of a counterfet religion, to laie hands on others kingdomes, and to snatch away the substance of other peoples.' The upshot of the pamphlet is that the Italians devised the domination of the Pope in order to carry to Rome the 'Quintescence of the peoples

[1] London, Printed by Iohn Wolfe, 1591. Dedicated to Henry IV of France and signed at the end with the initials G. B. A. F. The author of this pamphlet shows acquaintance with the *Discorsi*. Some of his opinions seem to be conceived in opposition to Machiavelli's. So what he says about Romulus and Numa is antithetic to Machiavelli's chapters on those kings (*Disc.* i. ix, xi). While Machiavelli (ch. xii) suggests to transfer the Holy See to Switzerland, in order to verify its deleterious effect on the country in which it is established, the author of the pamphlet (ch. vi) would persuade the Pope 'to come into Swicerland, and into France, verie curteous and good people: to deliver themselves from the yoake of that nation which is the most corrupt in the whole world'. (See also Gentillet, *cit. infra*, p. 224.)

[2] A theory, so far as I know, held true to this day by the Italians themselves. Michelangelo says: 'Se io ho nulla di buono nell' ingegno, egli è venuto dal nascere nella *sottilità dell' aria* d'Arezzo.' And Leopardi: 'I più furbi per abito e i più ingegnosi per natura di tutti gl'italiani sono i marchegiani; il che senza dubbio ha relazione colla *sottigliezza della loro aria*.'

purses': this money, once transported there, 'doth flie with an incredible swiftnesse'. 'It is our money they want'—so sounds the outcry of the huguenot writer, who knew only too well how to wield the most popular of all arguments. The remedy he proposed was to 'shut up from Italians al accesse or entrance into our Countrey', following 'the good instruction that nature and the Author therof doth set before us visibly' by his 'having laid and set the Alpes most high mountaines, so firme and permanent on the one side, and the deepe Seas on the other, for bars betweene us and them, that we should not go to one another'. If only the foreign nations, for their part, had respected those natural barriers!

'A lively patterne of Italian subtiltie' is seen by the author of the pamphlet 'in the person of Katherine de Medicis, and her Florentine Counsell':

> 'Never were there so many died by poyson of Serpents and other venimous beasts, nor by the crueltie of Tygers, Lybbards, Crocodiles, Lynxes, Beares, and other devouring beasts, since the creation of the world, as by their tyrannous crueltie.' 'And he which would desire to know what is become of all these excessive heapes of mony levied in this kingdome: let him goe to Florence, to behold the sumptuous buildings which there have been erected by our ruine.'

The charge of avarice levelled at the Florentine favourites of Catherine de' Medici, those Florentines who had come 'like poor snakes into France' and were leaving it swimming in 'wondrous wealth', became part and parcel of the Machiavellian bugbear. Gentillet, in the preface to the First Part of his famous anti-machiavellian book, wrote:

> 'Nous voyons à l'œil et touchons au doigt l'avarice des Italiens [Machiavellistes] qui nous mine et ruine, et qui succe toute nostre substance, et ne nous laisse rien.'[1]

The French origin of the Elizabethan Machiavellian is made evident by his very covetousness. Marlowe's Barabas, that 'true Machiavel', is above all a monstrous miser. His money 'was not got without my means', Machiavelli says

---

[1] See on p. 173 a diverting passage on *Atheistes inventeurs d'impost*.

of him in the prologue, and, in a much-quoted passage in the Second Act ('As for my selfe, I walke abroad a nights'), Barabas enumerates the stratagems which have made him rich. Nothing could be less true to the historical teaching of Machiavelli, who warned his Prince to avoid, of all things, robbing his subjects, since, he says, man forgets earlier the death of his father than the loss of his patrimony (*Principe*, xvii). He had foreseen only too well what was going to happen: men would have probably never waged such a relentless war against his name if the Florentine courtiers of Catherine de' Medici had refrained from 'fetching the quintessence' out of the purses of the French people.

After Meyer's epoch-making essay[1] it has been assumed that Gentillet's *Contre-Machiavel* was the book which caused the anti-machiavellian feeling to spread over England. Gentillet's book was published in 1576 and circulated first in the Latin translation, which went through three editions during the sixteenth century, before Simon Patericke published in 1602 his English version, which had been made in 1577, immediately after the publication of the book. Patericke's Preface has been interpreted by Meyer as giving evidence that Machiavelli was not known in England before 1577. This inference cannot be maintained, since we find Machiavelli already mentioned with a sinister connotation in the Sempill Ballads referring to Scottish political events, before Gentillet's work was published in French.[2] In one of these poems, as early as 1568, we find William Maitland of Lethington, the Secretary of Mary Queen of Scots, styled 'this false Machivilian'; in another ballad, dated 1570, he is called 'a scurvie Schollar of Machiavellus lair'; in another, dated 1572, we hear of 'men

[1] *Machiavelli and the Elizabethan Drama*, von Edward Meyer, Weimar, 1897 (Litterarhistorische Forschungen, I. Heft).
[2] O. Ritter, in *Englische Studien*, xxxii, pp. 159–60, first called attention to these Ballads, without, however, drawing the consequences. The Ballads are printed in *Satirical Poems of the Time of the Reformation*, ed. by J. Cranstoun (S.T.S.), 1891–3. They bear the numbers ix, xxii, xxx, xlv.

of Machevillus Scuillis'; and finally, in a poem of 1583 Archbishop Adamson is called 'Matchewell'. In Buchanan's *Admonitioun* (1570) we read: 'Proud contempnars or machiavell mokkeris of all religioun and vertew'. The first of those ballads, dated 1568, is very interesting, since in it occurs for the first time in English literature the derivative form *Machivilian*, a form which seems to presuppose an advanced stage of the Machiavelli legend.[1] As a matter of fact Secretary Lethington, who is the butt of that ballad, was popularly nicknamed the 'Mitchell Wylie' or Machiavelli of Scotland. Given the close relations between Scotland and France, we will find it very natural that the Machiavelli legend, hatched in France among the huguenots under the rule of Catherine de' Medici, should have first found its way to Scotland and the Scottish Reformers. Moreover, Robert Sempill, to whose pen those ballads are due, was in Paris several times, and obviously was well versed in French political circumstances. Therefore, we may safely conclude that Gentillet's book was not the sole source for the English travesty of Machiavelli. That book, certainly, did much towards giving wide circulation to the Machiavellian scarecrow, and fixing its abiding characteristics, but the ground on which it fell had already been prepared to receive it.[2]

---

[1] Therefore Meyer's statement (p. 27) that Robert Greene in 1583 'was the first to make in popular literature an abstract noun of the Florentine's name' is not exact.

[2] E. Köppel, in *Eng. St.*, xxiv, pp. 108–18, has traced the sources of Gentillet's *Maximes*, which he read in Meyer. Much trouble would have been spared to him had he seen Gentillet's text, where most of the sources are given. For B. 3, see *Disc.* III. ii: 'La nostra Religione ha glorificato più gli uomini umili e contemplativi, che gli attivi. Ha dipoi posto il sommo bene nella umiltà, abiezione, nel dispregio delle cose umane; quell' altra lo poneva nella grandezza dell' animo, nella forza del corpo, e in tutte l' altre cose atte a fare gli uomini fortissimi . . . Questo modo di vivere adunque pare ch' abbi renduto il mondo debole, e datolo in preda agli uomini scellerati.' The source of B. 4, which Köppel could not trace, is in *Disc.* II. v: 'E chi legge i modi tenuti da San Gregorio, e dagli altri capi della Religione Cristiana, vedrà con quanta ostinazione e' perseguitarono tutte le memorie

By then Machiavelli had become a sort of rallying-point for whatever was most loathsome in statecraft, and indeed in human nature at large. The political devices he had studied in past history, in order to infer from those historical premisses the laws of a political science, were fathered upon him as if he had been not their expounder but their actual inventor. His original contribution to the theory of the modern state, his unprecedented method of study, could not be grasped by the contemporaries of the unfortunate Florentine. What they found in him was, as usual, what already existed, since the easiest and commonest way of reading books is to see in them what is already in ourselves. The political diseases Machiavelli had first studied scientifically were called after his name, as a physical disease is nowadays called after the doctor who has first described it: but Machiavelli was no more the inventor of Machiavellism

antiche, ardendo l'opere de' Poeti e delli Istorici.' The source of Maxim C. 5 is to be found in *Disc.* II. xix: 'E veramente simili città o provincie si vendicano contra il vincitore senza zuffa e senza sangue; perché riempiendogli de' suoi tristi costumi, gli espongono ad esser vinti da qualunque gli assalta.' Maxim C. 19 is a paraphrase of *Princ.* xviii: 'Si vede per esperienzia ne' nostri tempi quelli principi avere fatto gran cose . . . che hanno saputo con l'astuzia aggirare e' cervelli delli uomini.' Maxim C. 24 is to be paralleled with *Disc.* II. ix: 'Perché se io voglio fare guerra con un Principe, e fra noi siano fermi capitoli per un gran tempo osservati, con altra giustificazione e con altro colore assalterò io un suo amico che lui proprio.' Maxim C. 31 sums up *Disc.* I. iv; C. 35 is drawn from *Disc.* I. vii: 'Bisogna che i giudici siano assai, perché pochi sempre fanno a modo de' pochi.' Maxim C. 36 derives from *Disc.* I. lv: 'Di questi nobili sono piene Napoli, Roma, la Romagna e la Lombardia: onde nasce che ivi non è mai stata alcuna vera repubblica . . . perché tali generazioni d' uomini sono al tutto nemiche d'ogni civiltà . . . In Toscana, invece, si hanno le repubbliche . . . E tutto questo segue perché non vi sono in esse signori di castella.' In this last case Gentillet condenses Machiavelli no less than in B. 8 where the French 'Moyse usurpa la Judée, comme les Goths usurperent partie de l'Empire Romain' concentrates several passages from *Disc.* II. viii. Occasionally Gentillet's references are very vague. Such is the case of Maxims C. 13 and C. 15, which Gentillet grounds respectively on *Disc.* I. ix and on *Disc.* III. ii; iii.

than Graves is the inventor of Graves's disease. Machiavelli supplied a label, a *cliché*, for describing methods which had been in use since remote antiquity. One of the most popular of his maxims, on the combination of fox and lion necessary in a statesman, had been current since the classical times. The character of a despotic prince had been sketched by Aristotle, St. Thomas Aquinas, Savonarola, and many medieval and fifteenth-century writers in terms similar to those used by Machiavelli. With the difference that, whereas those writers described that character from an ethical standpoint, and therefore condemned it, Machiavelli studied it from a scientific point of view, as a system of actions and reactions operating in a moral vacuum. His shortcomings were those of all Renaissance people. The theocratic, collectivist ideals of the Middle Ages were being replaced by a conception of life based on the pre-Christian polity and the individuum. The new conception emphasized the plastic force of the individual at the expense of the surrounding atmosphere; the new hero stood out arrayed in the full glory of his strength, almost too intense to be real. The discovery of the individuum was parallel to the discovery of the nude: the draughtsmen were so engrossed in the study of the anatomy of their models that they drew the human body not as it appears to the eye but as it is known to be constituted to the scientific mind of the anatomist. Machiavelli's hero is the counterpart of the nudes painted by Signorelli or sketched by Leonardo: he is a scientific being, breathing in an element subtler than the sublunar air, no less metaphysical than the medieval man, but by an inverse process of exaggeration. The medieval man was too much of a man in the mass; the Renaissance man, on the other hand, was isolated as a self-sufficient unit, since a reaction must go its whole length before the balance is re-established. Machiavelli's point of view was so different from that of Aristotle, St. Thomas, and Savonarola, that he did not suspect that his description of the Prince might have read as a monstrous travesty of the traditional description of the tyrant. No wonder, then, that that description was calculated to impress short-sighted interpreters either as a moral enormity or as an ironical *double entente*. The scientific point of view is the great contribution of Machiavelli; once that missed, the rest was neither original nor new.

But his point of view was gaining ground among the thinkers of Renaissance. Montaigne[1] contemplated cases in which the Prince must 'quitter sa raison à une plus universelle et puissante raison', and disregard 'son devoir ordinaire', i.e. the current moral principles; even the medieval-minded and morally irreproachable Sir Thomas More, in a fit of anti-militarism, had caused the Utopians to adopt in war-time policies much more objectionable than those advocated by Machiavelli in *Discorsi*, Lib. III, C. xl ('Come usare la fraude nel maneggiare la guerra è cosa gloriosa'). And the poet whose chivalrous character, elevation of sentiment, and sense of duty and religion Professor Courthope[2] contrasts to Marlowe's exaltation of the Machiavellian principles—Edmund Spenser—did not scruple to adopt almost word by word the maxims laid down by Machiavelli in his *View of the Present State of Ireland*.[3]

On the other hand, it cannot be said that Machiavelli's system was solely based on the corrupt political conditions of Italy. There was no such opposition as that imagined by Macaulay between foreigners, brave and resolute, faithful to their engagements, and Italians destitute of courage and sincerity. As a matter of fact, the most perfect incarnations of the Machiavellian Prince were to be found among foreign rulers. King John, Henry IV, Richard III (who is caused to say by Shakespeare: 'I can . . . set the murderous Machiavel to school'), Queen Elizabeth (who actually wrote to James VI: 'I mind to set to school your craftiest

[1] *Essais*, Livre III, ch. i, De l'Utile et de l'Honneste.

[2] *History of English Poetry*, II. xii, p. 421.

[3] See E. A. Greenlaw, *The Influence of Machiavelli on Spenser*, in *Modern Philology*, vii, pp. 187 ff.

councillor'),[1] all of them English sovereigns, Louis XI of France, to quote only the most conspicuous instances, were much more cunning foxes than that desperate petty weasel Cesare Borgia, who, by the way, was no Italian either, but a Spaniard.

But in the same way as Machiavelli became a label for all sorts of political crimes, Italy was looked upon in the Renaissance as the fountain-head of all horrors and sins. Italy was no worse, in that respect, than the rest of Western Europe, but while other nations had not attracted the attention of foreign observers, Italy had appealed to them for many reasons. One of these reasons was the splendour of her civilization, but another, no less powerful, was the exotic appeal which first was awakened in Europe, as a general phenomenon, by Italian travel. Finally, there was the religious factor, in consequence of which Rome was considered by protestants the City of the Antichrist. All these elements combined together in creating the Elizabethan picture of a bloodthirsty, deceitful, impious, and picturesquely emotional Italy. Henceforth a tale of horror, to be popular, had to be staged in Italy,[2] just in the same way as, until quite recently, a singer had to parade a fictitious Italian name, in order to attract public attention. I will quote one instance only of the *passe-partout* quality possessed by the Italian frame, because it is related to our present subject, Machiavelli. In *The Dutchesse of Malfy*, III. v, Ferdinand writes a letter in which occurs the expression: 'Send Antonio to me; I want his head in a busines.' This phrase provokes from the Duchess the following remark:

[1] See W. Alison Phillips, *The Influence of Machiavelli on the Reformation of England*, in *Nineteenth Century* for Dec. 1896, pp. 907–18.

[2] So Massinger, in *The Duke of Milan*, substitutes the Duke of Milan and his wife Marcelia for Herodes and Mariamne of his source. This Italianization was not confined to tales of horror. Massinger, again, dramatized an old English legend in his *Great Duke of Florence*. Jonson, in the first version of *Every Man in his Humour*, indulged the taste of the public and gave to the plot an Italian setting which a mere change of names showed to be only a thin veneer.

A politicke equivocation—
He doth not want your councell, but your head.

We are going to see shortly how the word *politic* in this bad sense came to be an equivalent of *Machiavellian*. From all appearances, then, we are confronted with a piece of Italian Machiavellism. Mr. F. L. Lucas, who has recently prepared an admirable edition of Webster, does not give any source for this remarkable equivocation, but there is an historical source. The sovereign who is actually reported to have had recourse to that sleight is Louis XI of France, who, wanting to punish the Connétable, let him be assured that he knew his faithfulness, and asked him to come, because he 'wanted such a head'. Lodovico Guicciardini, from whose *Ore di Ricreazione* I have gathered this anecdote, concludes:

'Dipoi voltatosi a un segretario pian piano disse, egli è vero che io ho bisogno di quel capo, ma separato dal busto, et soggiunse chi non sa simulare non sa regnare.'[1]

So much is it true what is written in a Caroline pamphlet, *The Atheistical Politician*, that

'if we examine the Life of *Lewis* the 11th of *France*, we shall finde he acted more ill, than Machiavill writ, or for ought we know ever thought; yet he hath wisedome inscribed on his Tomb.'

But his politic equivocation had to be put in the mouth of an Italian in order to show off at its best.

The gross travesty which Machiavelli's political science underwent is well illustrated by the Elizabethan use of the word *politic*. Machiavelli's use of the corresponding Italian word *politico* is instanced in these passages from the *Discorsi*:

I. lv: 'quelle Repubbliche, dove si è mantenuto il vivere *politico* ed incorrotto.'

III. viii: 'Per altri modi s' ha a cercare gloria in una città corrotta, che in una che ancora viva *politicamente*.'

Politico, then, in Machiavelli means 'in conformity with sound rules of statecraft'. It has a merely scientific meaning,

[1] Cf. Commynes, *Mémoires*, ed. Calmette, II, pp. 74–5 (Livre IV, ch. xi).

and is opposed to *corrotto*, which is synonym to 'mis-governed'. There is no instance of the word being used in Italian in the sense of 'scheming, crafty'. The only cases, quoted by dictionaries, in which the word has the connotation of 'shrewd' are not earlier than the end of the seventeenth century. In French, *politique* must have possessed the meaning of 'shrewd' in the second half of the sixteenth century, though Littré is only able to quote that use of the word in an author as late as Pascal. In Corneille's *Mort de Pompée* (1641) the evil counsellor Photin is thus referred to: 'Un si grand politique est capable de tout' (ii. iii). And, further on (iv. ii): 'Ces lâches politiques / Qui n'inspirent aux rois que des mœurs tyranniques.' But the word, by itself, cannot have been invested with the sinister connotation it came to possess in English, otherwise the moderate party which arose in France about 1573, and regarded political reform more urgent than the religious question, would not have been styled *politique*.

In English we find the word *policy* with the meaning of 'device' as early as 1406, in Hoccleve, where the device resorted to by Ulysses to escape the danger of the Mermaids is called a *policie* (N.E.D.). By the middle of the sixteenth century *policy* is a synonym to 'sleight, trick'. In the marginal summaries of Robynson's translation of *Utopia*, in the second edition (1556), we find: 'bellum pecunia aut *arte* declinare', translated by 'either with money or by *pollicie* to avoyde warre'; 'aliquo *stratagemate*' rendered with 'by some *pollicie*'. Another instance is supplied by Jasper Heywood's translation of Seneca's *Troas* (1559), where the Lat. *dolos* (l. 569) is rendered as *pollecy*. In Studley's translation of *Agamemnon* (1566) *pollecie* corresponds to Lat. *fraude* (l. 207). Other similar instances may be quoted from Newton's *Seneca*. The word is often found coupled with 'sleight', as in the following instance from *The Mirror for Magistrates* (*King Malin*, x, edition of 1587, N.E.D.): 'Secretly by *pollecy* and sleight / Hee slewe mee.' In the translation of *Utopia*, 1556, we find the famous stratagem consisting in changing the landmarks on the shore in order to destroy the navies of the enemies styled 'a *politique* device' in the marginal summary, where the Latin has *stratagema*; in the seventh tragedy of the first lot of *The Mirror for Magistrates* (*Henry Percy Earle of Northumberland*, xii, published in 1559, but written a few years before) we find *polliticke* used in the same sense of 'cunning'. In the former of the last two instances there can hardly be a sinister moral connotation, since Thomas More did not condemn the Utopian stratagem: Utopians (and More with them) held war 'a thinge very beastelye', and victory got by stratagem a thing that 'no other lyvynge creature but onely man' could achieve, 'that ys to saye, by the myghte and puysaunce of wytte'.[1] In Bk. II, ch. ix, it is said that the Utopians 'do marvelouslye deteste and abhorre . . . deceite, and falshed, and al maner of lyes, as next unto fraude'. Evidently those stratagems were not liable to be described so.

But with the diffusion of Machiavellism *politic* became closely associated with the disreputable principles of the Florentine Secretary. One wonders whether it was the adoption of Machiavellian statecraft, which began in England at the time of Thomas Cromwell and Henry VIII, who has been styled 'Machiavelli's Prince in action', to cast the bad connotation on the word. It is a curious question, which does not allow of a definite solution, since the evidence of extant literature must not be relied too much upon: at any rate, the date given by the N.E.D. for the first appearance of the usage of *politic* in the sense of 'scheming' seems rather too late. The instance, from Lyly's *Euphues*

[1] More's distinction is not very different from that drawn by Machiavelli (*Princ.* xviii) between 'dua generazione di combattere', of which 'quello con le leggi' is 'proprio dello uomo', 'quello con la forza' is 'proprio delle bestie'. Both More's and Machiavelli's is the typical humanistic outlook on the superiority of the mind over brutal force. The common source is Cicero, *De Officiis*, I. ix. 34: 'Nam cum sint duo genera decertandi, unum per disceptationem, alterum per vim; cumque illud proprium sit hominis, hoc beluarum, confugiendum est ad posterius, si uti non licet superiore.'

(1580), runs: 'For greater daunger is ther to arive in a straunge countrey where the inhabitants be *pollitique.*' To link *politic,* in the sinister sense, with Machiavelli, was customary by the end of the sixteenth century. In Lodge's *Reply to Stephen Gosson's Schoole of Abuse* (1580) we read, for instance: 'I feare me you will be *politick* wyth Machavel.' As soon as the dramatists became haunted by the character of the Machiavellian knave, they began to use with an unprecedented frequency the words *policy* and *politic. The Spanish Tragedy* teems with stratagems: Viluppo, Lorenzo, Ieronimo, all make use of villainous tricks. Lorenzo never gets tired of speaking of his *policy* (III. iv. 38; x. 9); he is called 'too *pollitick*' by Bellimperia (III. x. 83), and in *The first part of Ieronimo* is caused to exclaim (I. i. 123): 'O sweete, sweete *pollicie,* I hugg thee'; and to advise (II. ii. 12): 'Sly *policy* must be youre guide.' In *Soliman and Perseda* Basilisco 'held it *pollicie* to put the men children/Of that climate to the sword' (I. iii. 87–8), and Piston says (I. iv. 17): 'Oh, the *pollicie* of this age is wonderfull.'

Marlowe's Machiavellian Jew of Malta (who also uses the word *policy* a dozen times) thinks it no sin to deceive Christians, since they are all deceivers (l. 393 f.):

> I *policie?* that's their profession,
> And not simplicity, as they suggest.

In *Edward II* Lancaster says to Kent (l. 1073 f.):

> I feare me, you are sent of *pollicie,*
> To undermine us with a showe of love.

In Webster's *White Divel* the Machiavellian Flamineo says (I. ii. 341 ff.):

> We are ingag'd to mischiefe and must on.
> As Rivers to finde out the Ocean
> Flow with crooke bendings beneath forced bankes,
> Or as wee see to aspire some mountaines top,
> The way ascends not straight, but Imitates
> The suttle fouldings of a Winters snake,
> So who knowes *policy* and her true aspect,
> Shall finde her waies winding and indirect.

In that tragedy Camillo dies 'by such a *polliticke* straine,/ Men shall suppose him by's owne engine slaine' (II. i. 312–13). His fate is called 'a farre more *polliticke* fate' (II. ii. 35) than that of Isabella, who dies by kissing a poisoned picture. Marcello says to Flamineo (III. i. 60):

> For love of vertue beare an honest heart,
> And stride over every *polliticke* respect,
> Which where they most advance they most infect.

Like Ieronimo in *The Spanish Tragedy*, who had cunningly dissembled madness in order to further his revenge, Flamineo (III. ii. 318) thinks it advisable to 'appeare a *polliticke* madman'; swindlers who cheat their creditors are called (IV. i. 54) '*pollitick* bankroupts'; feigned ignorance is styled (IV. ii. 82) '*politicke* ignorance'. Lodovico and Gasparo whisper to dying Brachiano (V. iii. 155–6):

> You that were held the famous *Pollititian*;
> Whose art was poison. And whose conscience murder.

And, as in a litany, they draw a picturesque list of poisons, and conclude (ibid. 165–6):

> With other devilish potticarie stuffe
> A-melting in your *polliticke* braines.

The sinister use of the words *politic, policy, politician* may be illustrated with many other instances from Webster (none of them included in the N.E.D.); a characteristic one is found in *The Dutchesse of Malfy* (III. ii. 371 ff.), where Bosola says:

> A *Polititian* is the divells quilted anvell,
> He fashions all sinnes on him, and the blowes
> Are never heard.

The word *politician* is already found with a bad connotation in Nashe's *Pierce Penilesse his Supplication to the Divell* (1592): 'The Divel . . . was . . . so famous a *Polititian* in purchasing'; and in *The Unfortunate Traveller*: 'Hee set his cap over his ey-browes like a *polititian*, and then folded his armes one in another, and nodded with the head, as who would say, let the French beware for they shall finde me a divell.' In Middleton's *Game at Chess* (1624), where the words *politic*, *policy* recur frequently, the Black Knight, i.e. the Spanish

Ambassador Gondomar, is put into the bag with these words (v. iii. 201–2):

> Room for the mightiest *Machiavel-politician*
> That e'er the devil hatch'd of a nun's egg !

And W. Raleigh (*Maxims of State* in *Remains*, 1661, p. 46) has 'a cunning *Polititian,* or a Machiavilian at the least'. In most of the above instances the word *politician* is closely associated with the Devil: this very remarkable association ought to be kept in mind for what I shall say later on. A passage in John Day's *Humour out of Breath* (1607-8) conveys well the Elizabethan notion of *policy* (ii. i):

Aspero. How long have you bin a matchiavilian, boy?

  Boy. Ever since I practis'd to play the knave, my lord.

  Asp. Then *policy* and knavery are somewhat a kin.

  Boy. As neere as penury and gentry: a degree and a half remov'de, no more.

The word *statist* underwent a similar disparagement. In an instance of 1584 (N.E.D.) we read: 'When he plais the *statist*, wringing veri unlukkili some of Machiavels Axiomes to serve his Purpos.' In another instance of 1600 (N.E.D.) a Jesuit who intermeddles in state affairs is called a *statist*. The association between *politic* and *Machiavellian* became so close that actually the Italian form *politico* was used in England with the bad connotation already illustrated (see N.E.D. under *politico*). The discredit cast on the Florentine reflected on all the words connected with the art of government.

The dramatists were chiefly responsible for giving currency to the legend. A very interesting point is this: why did the dramatists adopt so eagerly the Machiavellian type of knave? How did Machiavelli become such an important character in the Elizabethan drama? Here is one of the vital points in the complex net of influences at work in the development of the Elizabethan drama: a point which, so far as I know, has not yet been illustrated. Among the stock characters bestowed by Seneca upon the tragedy of Renaissance was that of the cruel villainous tyrant, with his ambitious schemes and unprincipled maxims of government. Atreus is the most completely portrayed among the Senecan villains. He expounds his creed in a dialogue with his attendant.

Atreus has just disclosed his projects of cruel revenge against his brother, and the attendant asks (*Thyestes*, ll. 204 ff.)

Satelles.   Fama te populi nihil
            adversa terret?

Atreus.   Maximum hoc regni bonum est,
            quod facta domini cogitur populus sui
            tam ferre quam laudare.

Sat.   Quos cogit metus
            laudare, eosdem reddit inimicos metus.
            At qui favoris gloriam veri petit,
            animo magis quam voce laudari volet.

Atr.   Laus vera et humili saepe contingit viro,
            non nisi potenti falsa. quod nolunt velint.

Sat.   Rex velit honesta: nemo non eadem volet.

Atr.   Vbicumque tantum honesta dominanti licent,
            precario regnatur.

Sat.   Vbi non est pudor
            nec cura iuris sanctitas pietas fides,
            instabile regnum est.

Atr.   Sanctitas pietas fides
            privata bona sunt, qua iuvat reges eant.

Lycus, in *Hercules Furens*, corresponds to Machiavelli's 'principe nuovo'. He says (ll. 337 ff.):

                    nobiles non sunt mihi
            avi nec altis inclitum titulis genus,
            sed clara virtus.

Machiavelli's 'principe nuovo' relies most on his own *virtù*. Lycus goes on:

                    rapta sed trepida manu
            sceptra obtinentur; omnis in ferro est salus:
            quod civibus tenere te invitis scias,
            strictus tuetur ensis.

Therefore Lycus, in order to set his power on firm foundations, decides to marry Megara, from whose noble line his newness (*novitas nostra*) shall gain richer hue (the very device adopted by Richard III). But if Megara refuses, he is determined to ruin the whole house of Hercules:

> invidia factum ac sermo popularis premet?
> ars prima regni est posse invidiam pati.
>
> (ll. 352–3.)

And elsewhere (ll. 489; 511 ff.):

> Quod Iovi hoc regi licet.
>
> .   .   .   .
>
> Qui morte cunctos luere supplicium iubet
> nescit tyrannus esse. diversa inroga:
> miserum veta perire, felicem iube.

In the spurious *Octavia* Nero expounds to Seneca most of the same principles expounded by Atreus to his attendant. Among the rest, lines 456 ff. are noticeable:

> *Nero.*   Ferrum tuetur principem.
> *Seneca.*   Melius fides.
> *Ner.* Decet timeri Caesarem.
> *Sen.*   At plus diligi.
> *Ner.* Metuant necesse est—
>
> .   .   .   .   .
>
> Respectus ensis faciet.
>
> .   .   .   .   .
>
> tollantur hostes ense suspecti mihi.
>
> .   .   .   .   .   .
>
> quicquid excelsum est cadat.

In the *Phoenissae* (*Thebais*) the tyrant's part is played by Eteocles (ll. 654 ff.):

> Regnare non vult esse qui invisus timet:
> simul ista mundi conditor posuit deus,
> odium atque regnum: regis hoc magni reor,
> odia ipsa premere. multa dominantem vetat
> amor suorum; plus in iratos licet.
> qui vult amari, languida regnat manu.
>
> .   .   .   .   .   .
>
> Imperia pretio quolibet constant bene.

No doubt the author of the Induction to *A Warning for Faire Women* (1599) was right, when as a first characteristic of the Senecan drama he ranked:

> How some damn'd tyrant to obtain a crown
> Stabs, hangs, impoisons, smothers, cutteth throats.

It is a well-known fact that the Senecan tragedy reached England first through the Italian imitations. The characteristic type of the Italian Senecan drama was created by G. B. Giraldi Cinthio, and reigned supreme from 1541 to 1590. I need not repeat here what has been exhaustively illustrated by H. B. Charlton.[1] Almost all plots of the Italian Senecan drama can be described as instances of the contrast between a villain, usually a sovereign who is enabled by his position to exert his power for his private ends, and a heroine. What concerns us here is the type of the villain.

Now, when we come to examine closely Cinthio's characters falling under that description, we find that he developed the type of superhuman knave he found in Seneca with the help of elements derived from Machiavelli. Chiefly the character of Acharisto in *Euphimia* already possesses all the requisites of the Machiavellian bugbear of the Elizabethan stage. He is an aspiring villain who, through marrying Euphimia, daughter of the Corinthian king, has occupied the throne. He wants to enlarge his state by marrying the daughter of the king of Athens, and therefore, in order to get rid of Euphimia, accuses her of adultery: he adopts the same policy followed by the Senecan Lycus and by King Richard III. Here are some of his maxims:

> a me basta
> Ch' io sia, non men che Dio, da' miei temuto
> (II. i.)
> Il mio Dio è il mio volere, et ove questo
> Mi guida, i' voglio andare.
>
> .   .   .   .   .   .
>
> Che dee far altro un re, che cercar sempre
> Di far maggior lo stato, di acquistarsi
> Maggior potenza? tema la ragione
> Chi pover si ritrova, a sé è ragione
> Un possente signor, sia mal, sia bene
> Ciò che di fare a lui viene in pensiero,

[1] In the Introduction to *The Poetical Works of William Alexander*, Manchester, 1921.

Pur ch' utile vi sia, che vi sia acquisto,
Non dee lasciar mai di condurlo al fine.
Nessun cerca per qual modo, o qual via
Tu sia possente, o sia fatto signore,
Il tutto è haver, habbilo a dritto, a torto,
Come ricco tu sei, tu sei pregiato.
Filippo, Re di Macedonia, venne
Col non servar mai fé, con l' usar froda,
Col non attender mai cosa promessa,
Signore, in pochi dì, di tutta Grecia.

   .   .   .   .   .   .

Disse Lisandro, ch' ove non giungea
Il cuoio del Leon, vi si deveva
La pelle aggiunger d' una volpe. Io dico
Ch' ove giunger non puote la virtute
Cercar tu dei, che vi ti meni il vitio.
Che, quando tu acquistata hai la potenza,
Il vitio di virtù tiene sembianza.[1]
E, benché tu sia reo, tu sia malvagio,
Non manca chi ti dà lode infinite.   (II. ii.)

Apart from the general Senecan tone, this passage seems to show the influence of Machiavelli's both eighteenth chapter of *The Prince* and thirteenth chapter of the Second Book of the *Discorsi*. In the former is quoted the famous passage from Plutarch's *Lysander*, in the latter we read:

'Né credo si truovi mai che la forza sola basti, ma si troverà bene che la fraude sola basterà; come chiaro vedrà colui che leggerà la vita di Filippo di Macedonia.'

In the same drama (v. ii) one of the *consiglieri* expounds another passage from the eighteenth chapter of *The Prince*, which runs:

'Et hassi ad intendere questo, che uno principe, e massime uno principe nuovo, non può osservare tutte quelle cose per le quali li uomini sono tenuti buoni, sendo spesso necessitato, per mantenere lo stato, operare contro alla fede, contro alla carità, contro alla umanità, contro alla religione.'

---

[1] Cf. Marston's *Malcontent*, v. ii: 'Mischief that prospers men do virtue call.' Ben Jonson's *Catiline*, III. ii: 'and slip no advantage/That may secure you. Let them call it mischief;/When it is past and prospered 'twill be virtue.'

The *consigliere* in Cinthio's drama says:

> concedianvi, che la novitade
> De gli stati fa far cose a' Signori,
> Sian boni pur, sian quanto voglian giusti,
> Che non le fanno poi, che confirmati
> Sono nel Regno, e come è da lodare
> Novo Signor, che tenga gli occhi aperti,
> E cerchi servar sé, servar lo stato,
> Dando gran pena, dando agro castigo
> A chi nascosto gli apparecchia insidie,
>
> . . . .
>
> Così indegn' è, ch'un Re si dia a far male
> A chi Signor l'ha fatto, quando alcuna
> Cagion data non gli ha di fargli offesa.

The latter part reproduces a sentence in the twenty-first chapter of *The Prince*, concerning the debt of gratitude owed to the Prince by those who have achieved victory through his support: 'Li uomini non sono mai sì disonesti, che con tanto esemplo di ingratitudine ti opprimessino.'

In *Orbecche* the tyrant Sulmone, who holds fear to be the 'colonna dei regni', and 'n' ha sotto la fé mille traditi' (v. ii), has recourse to dissimulation in order to achieve the revenge he has planned. In *Altile* (which is based on *Hecatommithi*, ii. iii) the villainous Astano, who, by the way, is no king, but a simple nobleman, ruins Norrino by his treacherous simulation. His delight in making white look black is paralleled only by that of Iago, a character, we must remember, invented first by Cinthio: but we shall have to speak of Iago farther on. Astano, following the Senecan convention, discloses his mind to an attendant (i. iv):

> se fusse puro
> Questi via più che candida Colomba,
> Io lo farei parere un nero Corbo.
> Et se fusse Lamano la pietade
> Istessa, et la clemenza, io vo' che pensi
> Che col mio ingegno, più d'un Neron crudo
> (Poi ch'egli ha cominciato a darmi orecchio),
> Il farei divenire.

This is the very policy adopted by Iago with Othello. Like

Iago, Astano boasts the power of his words and guiles ('che potenza sia/Ne le parole mie, ne le mie insidie'):

> Vuoi tu, che il finger ti succieda? fingi
> Fede, et amor, et sotto habbi il coltello
> A dar l'ultimo colpo a chi ti crede,
> Sì tosto, che l'occasion ti s'offra.

Of his treacherous guiles Astano feels no more remorse than Iago, and for similar reasons:

> Né di questo debbo io biasimo havere,
> Havendomi intercetta ei la mia speme.

Astano, in fact, had vainly loved Altile, much in the same way as Iago, in Cinthio's tale, had vainly loved Desdemona. Astano is represented as gnawed by envy:

> Mi sentia roder da la Invidia, come
> Ruggine rode il ferro.

He promises (IV. ii) to be as solicitous of the ruin of Norrino as a mother is of the life of her own child:

> Non dubbitar, che non fu mai sì intenta
> A la salute del suo figlio madre,
> Quant'io a la costui morte sarò intento.

Astano actually succeeds in showing to the king, who at first threatens him, the two lovers together, whereas Iago merely stages an appearance of offence. One of the other characters says of him:

> O perché lasci, Giove,
> Vivere in terra un huom tanto malvagio?

Not only, then, do we find in Giraldi Cinthio the Senecan tyrant brought up to date on the lines supplied by *The Prince*, but also the maxims of villainous conduct, which Seneca had only put in the mouths of princes, become the property of a private person, a mere subject. Cinthio provides the link between the Senecan tyrant and the Elizabethan villain. His intentions—as Charlton says—had much in common with those of the Elizabethans, though he was devoid of all creative power and depth of human insight.

When we have become fully aware of Cinthio's intermediate position, then a whole ingenious and seemingly plausible theory of Vernon Lee on the Italians of the Renaissance needs qualification. Vernon Lee, in a well-known essay included in *Euphorion*,[1] maintains that the Renaissance Italians 'rarely or never paint horror or death or abomination', that 'the whole tragic meaning was unknown to the light and cheerful contemporaries of Ariosto'—whereas we know that Giraldi Cinthio was the first to interpret as *horrore* the φόβος Aristotle required for tragedy, and to give to the Thyestean banquet that widespread popularity we find recorded not only in the plays themselves, but also in such descriptions of their effect on the audience as Cinthio's in his *Discorso intorno al comporre delle commedie e delle tragedie*. On the ground of her gratuitous assumption, Vernon Lee actually built a theory on the amorality of the Renaissance Italians as contrasted with the maturer ethical judgement of the contemporary English—pushing to its extreme consequences the ideas expounded in Macaulay's essay on Machiavelli:—'They did not know how wicked they were.' Suppose they did not; but, then, neither did the Englishmen of the period. Since, in the same way as the Italian Senecans placed their gruesome plots among barbarian peoples, the English dramatists chose for the favourite scene of their horrors 'the darkened Italian palace, with its wrought-iron bars preventing escape; its embroidered carpets muffling the footsteps; its hidden, suddenly yawning trap-doors; its arras-hangings concealing masked ruffians; its garlands of poisoned flowers'—as Vernon Lee very picturesquely puts it. To the Italians 'oriental themes above all presented greater opportunities for gruesome horror and spectacular luxury, and especially those depicting the Turks of their own generation, even then hammering at Italy's gates'.[2] The same exotic touch was supplied to the Italians by oriental history, to the English by Italian

[1] *The Italy of Elizabethan Dramatists.*
[2] Charlton in the Introduction mentioned above, p. lxxxix.

contemporary events: romance is more appealing when staged against an exotic background. The exotic appeal is the main reason why Italians chose to dramatize the story of some unfortunate Armenian or Persian couple of lovers rather than the pathetic but too familiar story of the Duchess of Amalfi; the same exotic appeal which led English dramatists to write on the Duchess of Malfy or Bianca Cappello rather than to seek for their subjects at home, as they did in fact occasionally, in such dramas as *A Warning for Faire Women*, *Arden of Feversham*, and *The Yorkshire Tragedy*.

The Senecan drama was, then, the medium through which the Machiavellian principles, distorted as they had been, came to be uttered from the stage. Machiavellism, as epitomized by Gentillet, provided an up-to-date equipment of ideas to the worn-off classical tyrant; just as the essays of Montaigne supplied the dramatists with meditative passages, when the Senecan aphorisms began to sound too hackneyed. But the very fact that Machiavellism was merely grafted on a pre-existent Senecan type ought to warn us to be very cautious against detecting it everywhere, as Wyndham Lewis has recently done in his book on *The Lion and the Fox*. According to Mr. Lewis, 'the master figure of Elizabethan drama is Machiavelli . . . he was at the back of every Tudor mind.' But Seneca was at the back of every Tudor mind much more than Machiavelli, and sometimes what may be construed as Machiavellism is merely Senecan.

Senecan is, for instance, the tyrant Tancred in *Tancred and Gismund*, who is partly modelled on Giraldi Cinthio's Sulmone (in *Orbecche*); but to Simpson[1] Tancred seemed the first Machiavellian of the Elizabethan stage. Senecan is Marlowe's Tamburlaine, in whom Professor Brandl[2] imagined to discover many traits in common with Machiavelli's Prince. But the type of Tamburlaine is Seneca's Hercules:

[1] *The Political Use of the Stage in Shakespeare's Time.*
[2] *Gött. Gel. Anz.* 1891, no. 18, pp. 717 ff.

curiously enough, nobody seems to have noticed it. Tamburlaine proclaims several times to be a scourge of God, God's viceregent who executes tyrannies 'enjoin'd . . . from above, / To scourge the pride of such as Heaven abhors' (2 *Tamb*. ll. 3820 ff.). Seneca's Hercules (in *Herc. Oetaeus*, l. 1143) had said to Jupiter: 'Ille qui pro fulmine / tuisque facibus natus in terris eram.' Tamburlaine's desperate appeals, when life forsakes him (2 *Tamb*., ll. 4434 ff.), are a counterpart of Hercules's lamentations while tortured by the burning shirt:

> What daring God torments my body thus,
> And seeks to conquer mighty Tamburlaine?

His amazement is modelled on Hercules's amazement in seeing himself, a conqueror of the world, killed by a mysterious enemy (ll. 1161 ff.): 'Ego qui relicta morte . . . ego quem deorum regna senserunt tria / morior . . . sine morte vincor.'[1] Both challenge Death; Tamburlaine: 'See where my slave, the uglie monster death . . . ' (2 *Tamb*., l. 4459); and Hercules (ll. 1249 ff.): 'Quaecumque pestis viscere in nostro late / procede . . .' (l. 1373): 'invade, mors, non trepida . . .'; Tamburlaine's speeches are as full of hyperboles as Hercules's. Professor Brandl has thought Tamburlaine's wooing of Zenocrate a piece of Machiavellian policy, to be matched only by Richard III's proposal to Lady Anne, but Zenocrate is rather a counterpart of Iole in *Hercules Oetaeus*: she is, like her, the prisoner daughter of a king; she yields, like her, to the mighty conqueror. Tamburlaine is in so far an incarnation of Machiavelli's Prince, as he is a type of the self-confident superhuman hero, whose aspiring mind concentrates upon the attainment of a mundane end. But so is Hercules, in whom, besides, we find that craving after immortality which is also behind the vague, boundless aspirations of Tamburlaine.

[1] Tamburlaine compares himself to Alcides in 2 *Tamb*. iv. iii (l. 3991 of the whole play): 'The headstrong Iades of Thrace, Alcides tam'd . . . Were not subdew'd with valour more divine.'

The error of Professor Brandl (followed, here, by Court-hope) in setting down to Machiavellism the superhuman *virtù* of Tamburlaine has been repeated by Wyndham Lewis in the case of another hero of the class of Marlowe's colossus, a hero who might be described as his issue—Chapman's Duke of Byron. At a first superficial impression, the Duke of Byron may indeed strike one as 'affording a spectacle of a Machiavel in the making'—as Wyndham Lewis puts it—but that first impression is dispelled as soon as we study Byron in the light of the recent researches of Professor Schoell, who shows to us Chapman spell-bound by the 'moralized' image Plutarch had sketched of Alexander.[1] Machiavelli did never supply a pattern of heroism for the Elizabethan dramatists: such figures as Tamburlaine and Byron were expressions of the same spirit of *Wille zur Macht* which produced *The Prince*, but they did not derive from it directly.[2] Machiavelli only supplied characteristics of the politic villain, who, from the very beginning, was loathed at the same time as ridiculed.

It is a mistake to try to distinguish between different stages of the figure of the Machiavellian in Elizabethan drama.[3] There is no first period in which Machiavelli provides a type of heroic, unprincipled individualism, discredited in a successive stage by puritan morality. And it would be impossible to say when the Machiavellian knave, from being an object of horror, turns into an object of derision. As early as 1597 we find a caricature of the Machiavellian in the 'ugly mechanicall Captain' of Nashe's *Unfortunate Traveller*, who, persuaded by Jack Wilton that

[1] F. L. Schoell, *Études sur l'Humanisme continental en Angleterre*, Paris, 1926, p. 85.

[2] Such is also the case of Milton's Satan, in whom Professor Court-hope (*Hist. Engl. Poet.*, iii, pp. 415–16) has seen the embodiment of Machiavellian *virtù*. But aspiring pride had been a traditional feature of Satan, and the new touches added by Milton are rather to be traced back to Aeschylus's Prometheus than to Machiavelli's hero.

[3] As R. Fischer does in *Anglia-Beiblatt*, viii (May 1897—April 1898), p. 355.

he is a 'myraculous polititian', deserts from the English to the French, but, given away by his own foolishness, is flogged back to the English, who flog him in their turn. Other Machiavellian dupes are Chapman's Gostanzo in *All Fools* (about 1604) ('these politicians . . . are our most fools'—III. i), and Beaumont and Fletcher's Lucio in *The Woman Hater* (*c.* 1606). In Ben Jonson's *Volpone* (1606) the character of the Italianate Englishman Sir Politick Would-be is meant for a humorous skit at the Machiavellian fop. Like Machiavelli himself, Sir Politick loves 'to note and to observe', and, though he lives free from the active torrent, he marks 'the currents and the passages of things', for his own private use, and knows 'the ebbs and flows of state'. He thinks Ulysses a poor wit,[1] and sees plots and tricks of state everywhere. His wife has come with him to Venice 'for intelligence/Of tires and fashions, and behaviour/ Among the Courtezans': 'the spider and the bee suck from one flower', i.e. both are trained at the Italian school of manners. Sir Politick proves a very gullible simpleton, and is easily made a laughing stock. Ben Jonson ridiculed again the Machiavellian statesman in the character of Bias, 'a vi-politic, or sub-secretary', in *The Magnetic Lady*. A caustic caricature of the politician is found in *Alphonsus, Emperor of Germany*, a play which, though only performed in 1636, was written, possibly by a John Poole (not, of course, by Chapman), 'not much later than the epoch-making work of Marlowe' (Parrott). The secretary Lorenzo de Cyprus who, after having dictated to Alphonsus a grotesque epitome of *The Prince* derived from Gentillet, Phalaris-like, falls a victim to his own arts, and is poisoned with his own poisons, in accordance with his rules of policy, is an evident parody of Machiavelli. As Lorenzo is a caricature of Machiavelli, so Alphonsus is modelled on the historical Cesare Borgia, whom a false report described as Machiavelli's disciple. The banquet at which Alphonsus

[1] Cp. *3 Henry VI*, III. ii. 189: 'I'll . . . Deceive more slyly than Ulysses could.'

(who, like the Borgias, is a 'viperous, bloodthirsty Spaniard') tries to poison his enemies is a repetition of Pope Alexander VI's famous feast, with the difference that Alphonsus only pretends to be poisoned himself.

In *Alphonsus*, as in most minor dramas, many influences are at work. There is a slight influence of *Richard III* (chiefly for religious hypocrisy: I. ii. 84 ff.), but the strongest influences are of Marlowe's *Jew of Malta*, and of *The Spanish Tragedy*, the two plays which gave birth to the type of the Machiavellian knave on the Elizabethan stage. Indeed the question of Machiavellian influence on Elizabethan drama is complicated by the influence of those two plays, which was still more far-echoing than it is thought. Very seldom the dramatists had a first-hand acquaintance with Machiavelli's writings; most of the time the villainous traits in the characters of their dramas are borrowed from Kyd's and Marlowe's Machiavellians: at the utmost, fresh illustration was derived from Gentillet.

So, for instance, Webster's Flamineo in *The White Divel* is a Machiavellian after Kyd's Lorenzo in *The Spanish Tragedy*: in both cases, the aim of their policy is the marriage of their sister to a powerful lord, an aim which leads them to murder in each case the person to whom the sister is engaged. Webster's Romelio, in *The Devils Law-Case*, is, on the other hand, clearly influenced by Marlowe's *Jew of Malta* (see III. ii. 1 ff.).[1] Muly Mohamet in Peele's *Battle of Alcazar*, Aaron in *Titus Andronicus*, Eleazar in *Lust's Dominion*, are all progeny of Barabas.

Marlowe certainly, and Kyd very likely, had a fair knowledge of Machiavelli's doctrines. There can be little doubt in the case of Marlowe, whom Greene rebuked for having imbibed the 'pestilent Machiavilian policie'. Marlowe had studied in Cambridge, where Machiavelli's writings were eagerly read: just a little time before he was entered at Corpus Christi College (1581), a Cambridge man, Gabriel Harvey, obviously influenced by Gentillet,

[1] See O. Schröder, *Marlowe und Webster*, Halle, 1907, pp. 8–11.

as Meyer has shown,[1] in a Latin poem (1578) had put in Machiavelli's own mouth (*Machiavellus ipse loquitur*) a denunciation of his policy which obviously supplied the model for the prologue of *The Jew of Malta*. Later on, in London, Marlowe had further opportunity of hearing Machiavelli's principles discussed by Walter Raleigh and his circle.[2]

But, so far as other dramatists are concerned, their villains are little more than further developments of the type as introduced to the stage by Kyd and Marlowe. The 'most thoroughly Machiavellian figure on the English stage' is, according to Professor Courthope, Iago, but the pedigree of this character is to be found in Giraldi Cinthio rather than in Machiavelli. When we read the source of *Othello*, the seventh *novella* in the third Decade of the *Hecatommithi*, we can hardly fail to notice how much more Machiavellian Cinthio's *alfiero* is than his English counterpart, Iago. The ensign, disregarding the faith pledged to his own wife (who is described in the story as a *bella et honesta giovane*) and the friendship and obligation towards the Moor, falls violently in love with Desdemona and, when he sees that his wooing is all in vain, plots the revenge. Cinthio's ensign cannot justify his behaviour through any provocation or slight suffered at the hands of the Moor; he is the ideal knave who, finding obstacles in the way of his perverse will, seeks revenge through deceit and treachery. This type of knave has been further developed by Giraldi Cinthio in his drama *Altile*, where Astano is the exact counterpart of the ensign of the *novella* of the Moor of Venice, and, as we have seen, anticipates in many respects Shakespeare's Iago. But Shakespeare's Iago appears to us much less of a knave, if we keep in mind that he is incensed by the public report that Othello has cuckolded him. 'The ostensible plot of the play'—says Wyndham Lewis—'is really the revenge of the

---

[1] Meyer cit., pp. 22–4.

[2] In *The Cabinet Council containing the chief Arts of Empire*, and in *The Prince or Maxims of State*, Raleigh is heavily indebted to the *Principe* and the *Discorsi*.

sex-vanity of a subordinate on his chief, the revenge taking the form of inspiring his chief with the same feelings of jealousy and wounded vanity that he has experienced himself.' On this account, Iago's story, as told by Shakespeare, finds parallels in many cases of retaliation instanced by Italian *novelle*: Iago, an accomplished Machiavellian demon in Cinthio, becomes much more human and excusable in Shakespeare. The reality of Iago's jealousy seems indeed to be doubted by some commentators. The lines (IV. i. 46–8):

> Thus credulous fools are caught:
> And many worthy and chaste dames even thus,
> All guiltless, meet reproach—

are commented upon, for instance, by H. C. Hart in *The Arden Shakespeare*, thus: 'These lines show the unreality of Iago's motives with which he formerly pretended to salve his conscience. He finds that he can ruin the happiness of innocent people. He can do it causelessly, and he is triumphant.' I would not lay so much stress on those lines, since they echo almost literally the moral of Cinthio's story:

> 'aviene talhora che senza colpa, fedele et amorevole donna, per insidie tesele da animo malvagio, et per leggierezza di chi più crede che non bisognerebbe, da fedel marito riceve morte.'

An extreme development of the character of the villain is found in Webster's Bosola, who partly reminds one of Iago, but of an Iago endowed with the melancholy and the wavering conscience of Hamlet: all the acts of this 'meditative murderer or philosophic ruffian'—as Swinburne calls him—are cursed, so that unwittingly he kills the very Antonio he meant to save 'above his own life'.

It has been doubted whether Shakespeare had direct access to Machiavelli's writings. Köppel[1] thought indeed he had discovered direct borrowings from Machiavelli in the portrait of King Claudius in *Hamlet*, but the parallels he quotes do not seem altogether cogent. The opinion about the awe-striking effect of the 'divinity' which 'hedges a king' was one so firmly established and widespread since

[1] See *Englische Studien*, xxiv, quoted above.

remote antiquity that it cannot be traced to any particular source. 'Politic' madness such as we find in *Hamlet* had first been employed on the stage by Kyd, in the character of Ieronimo. Kyd may have derived it from *Discorsi* III. ii: 'Come egli è cosa sapientissima simulare in tempo la pazzia.' What Machiavellism is displayed in Shakespeare's historical dramas seems either to be already present in the historical sources (as in the case of *Richard III*), or to be derived from the broadcast popular legend. In *3 Henry VI* Shakespeare wrote 'And set the murderous Machiavel to school' (III. ii. 193), where *The True Tragedy* has: 'And set the aspiring Catalin to schoole.' He was merely changing a label: the facts remained the same, with a new name. In *1 Henry IV* (I. iii. 285 ff.) Worcester says:

> For, bear ourselves as even as we can,
> The king will always think him in our debt,
> And think we think ourselves unsatisfied,
> Till he hath found a time to pay us home.

This seems indeed to reproduce very closely a passage in the third chapter of *The Prince* (the chapter from which Köppel derived the similitude drawn from the hectic fever in *Hamlet*, IV. iii. 67) about the founder of a *principato nuovo*:

> 'non ti puoi mantenere amici quelli che vi ti hanno messo, per non li potere satisfare in quel modo che si erano presupposto.'

But the similarity is still greater with a passage in *Leycester's Commonwealth* (1584) reproducing Machiavelli's maxim:

> 'For that such Princes, after ward can never give sufficient satisfaction to such friends for so great a benefice received. And consequently least upon discontentment, they may chance doe as much for others against them, as they have done for them against others: the surest way is, to recompence them with such reward, as they shall never after bee able to complain of.'

Indeed Machiavelli's text concludes that one cannot employ against friends *medicine forti*, 'sendo loro obligato'.

Ben Jonson had a direct acquaintance with Machiavelli's writings, as it appears from his *Discoveries*, from passages of the unfinished *Fall of Mortimer*, and from such occasional use of Machiavelli's terminology as in two passages of *Sejanus* (iii. i; iii. iii), where *fortune* and *virtue* are contrasted;[1] but, on the other hand, what in *Sejanus* might remind one of Machiavelli is, instead, almost literally borrowed from Seneca. So the dialogue about policy between Tiberius and Sejanus (ii. ii) is little more than a collection of the tyrant's maxims given by Seneca in *Thyestes*, *Thebais*, and *Octavia*. That Meyer, who ignored the Senecan origin of those maxims, could find parallels for them in Machiavelli's writings, shows once more how cautious one must be in the study of Machiavelli's influence upon the stage. Also Tamburlaine's disciple, Selimus, in the play of this name, is after the Senecan tyrant, and not after the Machiavellian Prince.

Of course, the Machiavellism of many minor characters in Elizabethan drama is unmistakable. Aspiring Guise in Marlowe's *Massacre at Paris*, Monsieur and Baligny in Chapman's *Revenge of Bussy d'Ambois*, Piero in Marston's *2 Antonio and Mellida*, Mendoza in *The Malcontent*, Latorch in *The Bloody Brother* (by Fletcher and Jonson, (?) revised by Massinger)[2] are admittedly Machiavellian; Barnes's *Divels Charter* is a thoroughly Machiavellian play by its very argument, Pope Alexander VI's story, which Barnes derived from Guicciardini and combined with Marlowe's version of the legend of Doctor Faustus. Allusion to Machiavellian policy is very frequent in all the authors of this period, as Meyer has shown in his patient and almost exhaustive *corpus* of quotations. But most of those quotations are echoing a popular *cliché*; their import does not reach beyond a superficial passing record of a fashionable byword: many authors using the word *Machiavellian* did not know about

---

[1] 'She herself [fortune], when virtue doth oppose,/Must lose her threats.' 'Men's fortune is their virtue.' A similar use of the binomial 'virtue-fortune' in Sidney's *Arcadia*. See S. L. Wolff, *The Greek Romances in Elizabethan Prose Fiction*, New York, 1912, pp. 326–7.

[2] See for authorship, E. H. Oliphant, *The Plays of Beaumont and Fletcher*, New Haven, 1927, pp. 457–63.

it more than most of us do while using to-day the word *bolshy*. On the other hand, in many authors acquainted with Machiavelli's writings, Machiavellism combined with other influences: most of the time, as I have shown, with the influence of Seneca; sometimes with that of the Greek romance, where dissimulation and stratagems were common enough: such is the case of the Machiavellian characters in Greene's novels: Pharicles, Arbasto, and Pandosto.[1]

In the cant use of the word, Machiavellism suggested chiefly two things: a treacherous way of killing, generally by poison; and atheism. A passage in Nashe's *Pierce Penilesse*[2] gives details about 'the arte of murther Machiavel hath pend' (*Summer's Last Will and Testament*, l. 1397):

> 'O Italie, the Academie of man-slaughter, the sporting place of murther, the Apothecary-shop of poyson for all Nations: how many kind of weapons hast thou invented for malice? Suppose I love a mans wife, whose husband yet lives, and cannot enioy her for his iealous over-looking: Physicke, or rather the

---

[1] See Wolff cit., p. 412. For Seneca see J. W. Cunliffe, *The Influence of Seneca on Elizabethan Tragedy*, London, 1893. (*Sejanus*, pp. 89 ff.) To the classics, rather than to Machiavelli, is also to be traced much of Corneille's 'Machiavellism'. The maxims of his villain Photin, in *La Mort de Pompée*, are borrowed from the speeches of Pothinus in Lucan, *De Bello Civ.* viii. 482 ff. But such device as, in *Polyeucte*, Félix suspects Sévère to employ against him (v. i), of letting him reprieve Polyeucte in order to ruin him utterly in the eyes of the Emperor, is eminently Machiavellian:

> Je sais des gens de cour quelle est la politique,
> J'en connais mieux que lui la plus fine pratique.
>
> .   .   .   .
>
> De ce qu'il me demande il me ferait un crime.

We find this device noted also in *Leycester's Commonwealth*: 'the Machiavilian sleight . . . of driving men to attempt somewhat, whereby they may incur danger, or remaine in perpetuall suspition or disgrace'. After Polyeucte has been sacrificed by Félix, too solicitous of his own safety, Sévère addresses him thus (v. vi):

> Père dénaturé, malheureux politique,
> Esclave ambitieux d'une peur chimérique.

[2] Ed. McKerrow, i, p. 186.

art of murther (as it may be used), will lend one a Medicine which shall make him away, in the nature of that disease he is most subiect to, whether in the space of a yeare, a moneth, halfe a yeare, or what tract of time you will, more or lesse.'

These Machiavellian poisons, punctual like clock-work, became no less of a regular property of the Elizabethan stage than the Senecan bloody blades. In *The Jew of Malta* we come across a precious powder bought at Ancona 'whose operation is to binde, infect, / And poyson deeply: yet not appeare / In forty houres after it is tane' (ll. 1373 ff.). In *Alphonsus Emperor of Germany*, out of that powder has grown a whole box of poisons, which is given to Lorenzo de Cyprus by Julius Lentulus, 'a most renowned Neapolitan'. Other Machiavellian tricks are expounded by Lightborn in Marlowe's *Edward II* (ll. 2363 ff.):

> I learnde in Naples how to poison flowers,
> To strangle with a lawne thrust through the throte,
> To pierce the wind-pipe with a needles point,
> Or whilst one is a sleepe, to take a quill
> And blowe a little powder in his eares,
> Or open his mouth, and powre quick silver downe,
> But yet I have a braver way then these.

This braver way, as it is shown afterwards, consists in holding the person down on the bed with a table, and stamping on it. Many of these picturesque devices were exploited by the most spectacular of all Elizabethan dramatists, Webster, who set great store on 'the rare trickes of a Machivillian'. His Flamineo says (*White Divel*, v. iii. 194 ff.):

> Those are found waightie strokes which come from th' hand,
> But those are killing strokes which come from th' head.
> O the rare trickes of a Machivillian!
> Hee doth not come like a grosse plodding slave
> And buffet you to death: no, my quaint knave—
> Hee tickles you to death; makes you die laughing;
> As if you had swallow'd a pound of saffron.

This passage is echoed by Middleton, in the *Game at Chess*, where the Black Knight, the Machiavellian Gondomar, says (i. i. 257 ff.):

> And what I've done, I've done facetiously,
> With pleasant subtlety and bewitching courtship,
> Abus'd all my believers with delight,—
> They took a comfort to be cozen'd by me:
> To many a soul I've let in mortal poison,
> Whose cheeks have crack'd with laughter to receive it.
>
> . . . .
>
> They took their bane in way of recreation.

As one sees from these and dozens of similar instances, the Elizabethans could never get over the excitement caused by the report of 'Borgias wine', though poisoning and wholesale murder were as rife in England as anywhere else in Renaissance Europe.

Diabolical atheism is another abiding feature of the mythical Machiavelli. The accusation dates from the first ecclesiastical campaign against *The Prince*. It will be remembered that already Cardinal Pole had called *The Prince* a book 'Satanae digito scriptum'. Gentillet did little else but give the finishing touch to the dark picture the Catholic clergy had been elaborating for half a century against the anticlerical writer, whose comparison between the Pagan and the Christian religion (in *Discorsi*, ii. ii) was purposely misconstrued into an atheistic argument. This accusation reflected on the popular account of Machiavelli's life. He was portrayed as a thoroughly bad and ignorant man, addicted to all vices, hating his country, banished from Florence (Gentillet), and dying in despair (Greene). They distorted his name in order to see in it an emblem of his villainy: he was called *Match a villain*, '*Mach-evill* that evill none can match' (Davies), *Hatch-evil*.[1] His Christian name got confused with the previously existing 'Old Nick' for the Devil.[2] Sometimes he was described as a new Simon Magus (George Whetstone, *English Myrror*, Lib. iii); he was

---

[1] Meyer cit., pp. 68–9, 116–17. The Jesuit Raynaud had first given currency to the legendary account of Machiavelli's death: 'blasphemans evomuit reprobum spiritum'.   [2] Meyer cit., pp. 93, 177 ff.

compared with Cain, Judas, Julian the Apostate (Greene, *Groat's Worth of Wit*). But the most fruitful side of the Machiavelli myth was the representation of the Florentine as an instrument of Satan, as ridden by an incubus, as the Secretary of Hell, as the Devil himself turned moralist.[1] So much did the terms Machiavelli and Satan become interchangeable that, whereas at first the tricks attributed to Machiavelli were called devilish, later on the Devil's own tricks were styled 'Machiavellian' (Nashe, *Terrors of the Night*). By an inversion of the process which had resulted in describing Machiavelli as a devil, the Devil himself became tinged with Machiavellism. On this later development I shall have shortly to say a few more words.

Since Machiavellism had become the common denominator for sins of every description, we will not be surprised in finding not only the Senecan tyrant dressed in the new Florentine garb, but also other old stock characters of drama brought up to date with Machiavellian trimmings. In Kyd's Lorenzo and in Webster's Flamineo we have Machiavel in the role of Pandar; in Barabas, Machiavel in the role of the Miser; in Iago, Machiavel in the role of the Revengeful Cuckold; and in Gostanzo (*All Fools*), Machiavel as the Gullible Father of the Terentian comedy.

Machiavelli's name is found coupled with that of the other Italian scandal, Aretino, and we come across the curious hybrid form *Mach-Aretines* (in Sylvester's *Lacrymae Lacrymarum*), we hear of *Aretines Politicks* (Glapthorne) and of *veneriall Machiavelisme* (Nashe);[2] and we find a prostitute called 'a Machiavel' (Thomas Andrew).[3] Better still, Machiavelli is associated with Ignatius Loyola, and we actually come across the monstrous combination *Ignatian Matchivell*.[4]

---

[1] Meyer cit., pp. 20, 53 f., 80 n. 1, 97 n. 3, 103 f.

[2] Meyer cit., pp. 119, 156; *Works of Nashe*, ed. McKerrow, ii, p. 153.

[3] Meyer cit., p. 102.

[4] In *Lines to the Bischopes*, attributed to Drummond of Hawthornden, ed. Kastner, ii, p. 293.

This latter contamination deserves to be illustrated, since it has not been noticed either by Meyer or by the others who have written on the Machiavelli legend. It may seem strange that the Jesuits, who were among the first and fiercest detractors of Machiavelli, to the point of having him burned in effigy at Ingolstadt as *cacodaemonis auxiliator*, should have become closely connected with him in the English mind. Still, we will understand how the bringing together of the two *bêtes noires* of the protestants became possible, if we bear in mind the character of the Society of Jesus.

The ultimate meaning of Machiavelli's doctrine had been a reassertion of terrene life and ideals against the ascetic conception of the Middle Ages, which placed the aim of human activities beyond earthly life. Against this theological outlook, Machiavelli had raised the ancient ideal of power acquired and enjoyed on earth. Against a humble and contemplative life, and the 'dispregio delle cose umane', leading men to submit themselves to their spiritual guides, Machiavelli had restored the dignity and beauty of things 'atte a fare gli uomini fortissimi' during their earthly life, and leading to the achievement of happiness on earth. To this aim he had made all the rest, even religion, subservient: he had adopted Gino Capponi's praise of those who love 'more their country than the salvation of their souls'.

Now, Jesuitism was as typical of the Renaissance as Machiavelli's political creed. Since the medieval ideals of humility and contemplation had been supplanted by a conception of life based on will of domination and active undertaking, the Jesuits transferred to the terrene plane the centre of the religious system, and made the glory of God coincide with the terrestrial power of their Society. Apart from the different denomination, their aim coincided with the aim for which Machiavelli stood—the achievement of supremacy on earth. Theirs was a defence of medieval theocracy with the very methods which had been devised to fight against it. In the same way as the Machiavellians

conceived all manifestations of spiritual life, first of all religion, as so many instruments of policy, so the Jesuits
adopted art, literature, in short all the appealing side of
Humanism, as instrumental to their aim of controlling men
and states. Domination was in both cases the chief aim:
everything else was degraded to the rank of tool, to be laid
aside when its function had been fulfilled. In both cases all
scruples had to be disregarded, whenever a certain action
was conducive to the aim, which in Machiavelli's case was
the glory of the country, in the case of the Jesuits the glory
of God. Political writers under Jesuit influence had in
fact so much in common with Machiavelli that, notwith-
standing their apparent anti-machiavellism, they actually
reproduced Machiavelli's principles while pretending to
derive them from Tacitus.[1]

Hence, in the popular report, the doctrines of both
Machiavelli and Loyola could be epitomized in the formula:
'the end justifies (or sanctifies) the means.' One of the
means of which the Jesuits made constant use was equivocation, which was a perfect counterpart of Machiavellian
dissimulation. Equivocation became a byword in England
since Henry Garnet, superior of the Jesuits in England,
used it during his trial for complicity in the Gunpowder
Plot. Therefore it was only too natural that the two chief
figures of the political and religious world of the South
should have been confused together by the Englishmen of
Queen Elizabeth's time, who had religious and political
causes of hatred against that nation which was the secular
arm of the Church—Spain. The Jesuited Politician became
the butt of the English people.

An adjective frequently used in connexion with both
Machiavelli and the Jesuits was *polypragmatic*, i.e. meddle-

[1] See G. Toffanin, *Machiavelli e il Tacitismo*, Padova, 1921. In this
book is also to be found an interesting chapter on 'Il Valentino e
Tiberio', where it is shown how much Tiberius, as portrayed by Tacitus,
had in common with Cesare Borgia. No wonder then if Meyer, in
reading Ben Jonson's *Sejanus*, was reminded of Machiavelli.

some. In the N.E.D. we find recorded: 'Polypragmaticke Papists', 'polypragmatic Machiavel', 'Iesuited Poly-prag-matiques', 'the most atheall Polypragmon Father Parsons'. From the last instance it appears that the accusation of atheism, raised against Machiavelli first of all by the Jesuits, had finally stretched also to them in the popular report. Polupragmaticus, 'Iesuita, Magus', &c., and Aequivocus, 'Iesuitae servus', are characters in Robert Burton's satirical play *Philosophaster* (1606): another character is the sophist Simon Acutus, whose nationality is Italian.

Polupragmaticus is heard teaching the other impostors of the play how to behave. Here is a passage of his dialogue with Simon:

> *Polu.* Tuum est disputare de Infinito, Ente, Vacuo
>
> . . . .
>
> De Gabrielitate Gabrielis, et spiritali anima.
> *Sim.* Vellem quod jubes si possem.
> *Polu.* Potes fingere, et mentiri, et hoc satis.
> *Sim.* Dabo operam.
> *Polu.* Ne dubites; unica virtus erit impudentia
>
> . . . . . .
>
> Suum cujusque curet officium.
> Ego meum, bilinguis, ambidexter, omniscius
> Jactabo quidvis, prout dabitur occasio,
> Callere me omnes linguas, artes, scientias,
> Nescire, aut haesitare, stolidum existimo.
> Sed verbo dicam Jesuitam prae me feram.
> *Sim.* Cur Jesuitam?
> *Polu.* Quid non audet hoc genus hominum
> In regum aulas, gynaecia, quo non ruit?
> Quod intentatum reliquit scelus?

Here the Jesuit is naïvely made the mouthpiece of the author, much in the way Machiavelli was caused to condemn himself in the prologue to *The Jew of Malta*. Later on the servant Aequivocus says of his master:

> qua non abit? huc, illuc, ubique,
> Per omnes vicos urbis noctivagus repit
> Ad horas omnes noctis, nunc virili habitu
> Nunc muliebri incedens, omnes formas induens,

Lenae, obstetricis, interdum vero militis,
Proteus opinor non est illo mutabilior,
Nec vulpes mage versipelles, aut versutior.

Here the Jesuit is represented as a fox. It was not long
before the famous Machiavellian saying on the lion and the
fox became applied also to him. Of such use we have a wit-
ness in one of the thirty-two *New and Choise Characters*
printed together with Overbury's poem *The Wife*: according to Mr. F. L. Lucas, Webster is possibly the author of
these *Characters*.[1] A Jesuit, we read there among other
things, 'in Rome, and other countries that give him free-
dome, . . . weares a Maske upon his heart; in England he
shifts it, and puts it upon his face. . . . To conclude, would
you know him beyond Sea? In his Seminary, hee's a Foxe;
but in the Inquisition, a Lyon Rampant.' And in a pamphlet of 1653 (*The Anabaptist Washt and Washt, &c.*, London,
Printed by William Hunt) we see in the frontispiece a half-
length figure of a Jesuit, with an open mouth similar to the
mouth of a lion's head facing him, and above we read the
words: 'Obrugiens Ore Leonino Vulpinus Iesuita.'

Ignatius Loyola and Machiavelli are both represented as
pleading at Lucifer's Court in John Donne's *Ignatius his
Conclave*, published in Latin and then in English in 1611.[2]
Donne has given to his pamphlet the form of a vision of hell.
He sees all the rooms in hell open to his sight, and, in
the innermost of them, Lucifer with a few chosen spirits.
Lucifer examines the titles of those who claim to be admitted to that secret place, a favour granted only to people
who have attempted great innovations, induced doubts
and anxieties and scruples, and at length established
opinions directly contrary to all established before. Ignatius
Loyola, who appears in the role of Lucifer's mentor, is

[1] *The Complete Works of John Webster*, ed. Lucas, iv, p. 42.
[2] In a print of 1605 on *The Powder Treason, Propounded by Sathan*, &c.
(Br. Mus. Cat., Political and Personal, i, n. 67) are pictured the Mouth
of Hell, the Devil holding a scroll, and numerous evil spirits, with the
words: 'Ignations Conclave'.

determined to oppose all claimants except those of his own order. After Copernicus's and Paracelsus's services have been proclaimed not sufficiently distinguished to raise them to so high a preferment in hell, Machiavelli is ushered in. Between Machiavelli and Loyola ensues a dispute which keeps enough satirical pungency to render it palatable even to modern readers. Machiavelli, seeing how Ignatius, uncalled, has thrust himself into the office of King's Attorney, and scorning as unfit for a Florentine the patience of the two preceding German claimants, thinks at first to get some venomous darts out of his Italian arsenal to cast against the worn soldier of Pampeluna, 'this *French-Spanish* mungrell', Ignatius. But, on perceiving how Lucifer approves whatever Ignatius says, he suddenly changes his purpose, and determines to direct his speech to Ignatius as to the principal person next to Lucifer, in order both to mollify him and to make Lucifer jealous and fearful lest Ignatius, 'by winning to his side politique men, exercised in civill businesses, might attempt some innovation' in his kingdom. Therefore he begins to speak thus:

'Dread *Emperour*, and you, his watchfull and diligent *Genius*, father *Ignatius*, *Arch-chancellor* of this *Court*, and highest *Priest* of this highest *Synagogue* (except the Primacy of the *Romane Church* reach also unto this place) let me before I descend to my selfe, a little consider, speake, and admire your stupendious wisedome, and the gouvernment of this state. You may vouchsafe to remember (great *Emperour*) how long after the *Nazarens* death, you were forced to live a solitarie, a barren, and an Eremiticall life: till at last (as it was ever your fashion to imitate heaven) out of your aboundant love, you begot this deerely beloved sonne of yours, *Ignatius*, which stands at your right hand. And from both of you proceedes a spirit, whom you have sent into the world, who triumphing both with *Mitre* and *Crowne*, governes your Militant Church there.'

Machiavelli goes on praising the art of equivocation:

'For my part (ô noble paire of *Emperours*) that I may freely confesse the truth, all which I have done, wheresoever there shall be mention made of the Iesuites, can be reputed but

childish; for this honor I hope will not be denied me, that
I brought in an *Alphabet*, & provided certaine Elements, & was
some kind of schoolmaister in preparing them a way to higher
understandings.'

Machiavelli has taught the Jesuits the rudiments of their
art: he is therefore indignant not to be admitted straightway
to the *sanctum sanctorum* of hell. If Paracelsus had some
claim to the Jesuits' favour because of his having been 'con-
veniently practised in the butcheries and mangling of men',
so much the more is Machiavelli entitled to that favour:

> 'For I my selfe went alwaies that way of bloud, and therefore
> I did ever preferre the sacrifices of the *Gentiles*, and of the *Iewes*,
> which were performed with effusion of bloud (whereby not only
> the people, but the Priests also were animated to bold enter-
> prises) before the soft and wanton sacrifices of *Christians*.'

This passage is almost a literal rendering of a passage in the
notorious second chapter of the Second Book of the *Discorsi*.[1]

> 'But yet although the entrance into this place—*goes on Machia-
> velli*—may be decreed to none, but to Innovators, and to onely
> such of them as have dealt in *Christian* businesse; and of them also,
> to those only which have had the fortune to doe much harme,
> I cannot see but next to the Iesuites, I must bee invited to enter,
> since I did not onely teach those wayes, by which, through *per-
> fidiousnesse*, and *dissembling of Religion*, a man might possesse, and
> usurpe upon the liberty of free *Commonwealths*; but also did arme
> and furnish the people with my instructions, how when they
> were under this oppression, they might safeliest conspire, and re-
> move a *tyrant*, or revenge themselves of their *Prince*, and redeem
> their former losses; so that from both sides, both from *Prince* and
> *People*, I brought an aboundant harvest, and a noble encrease
> to this kingdome.
> 'By this time—*says Donne*—I perceived *Lucifer* to bee much

---

[1] 'I Gentili . . . erano nelle azioni loro più feroci. Il che si può con-
siderare da molte loro constituzioni, cominciandosi dalla magnificenza
de' sacrifizii loro alla umiltà dei nostri, dove è qualche pompa più
delicata (Donne: *soft*) che magnifica; ma nessuna azione feroce o
gagliarda. Quivi . . . vi si aggiungeva l'azione del sacrifizio pieno di
sangue e di ferocia . . . il quale aspetto sendo terribile, rendeva gli
uomini simili a lui.'

moved with this Oration, and to incline much towards *Machiavel*. For he did acknowledge him to bee a kind of *Patriarke*, of those whom they call *Laymen*.'

Machiavelli is, therefore, a forerunner of those *Jésuites de robe courte* who were employed in the most risky missions, first of all in killing the sovereigns who opposed the plans of the Society. Donne is here adopting a theory advanced by Cardinal Pole, and repeated by Albericus Gentilis (*De Legationibus*, Lib. III, C. ix), according to which Machiavelli, under pretence of instructing the princes, was supposed to teach the subjects how to get rid of their tyrants.

'And therefore he [Lucifer] thought himselfe bound to reward *Machiavel*, which had awakened this drowsie and implicite *Laytie* to greater, and more bloody undertakings. Besides this, since *Ignatius* could not bee denied the place, whose ambitions and turbulencies *Lucifer* understood very wel, he thought *Machiavel* a fit and necessarie instrument to oppose against him; that so the skales beeing kept even by their factions, hee might governe in peace, and two poysons mingled might doe no harme.[1] But hee could not hide this intention from *Ignatius*, more subtil than the *Devill*, and the verier *Lucifer* of the two: Therefore *Ignatius* rushed out, threw himselfe downe at *Lucifers* feet, and groveling on the ground adored him.'

Ignatius proceeds to expose how much the 'obscure *Florentine*' has transgressed against Lucifer and the Pope his image-bearer, and last of all against the Jesuit Order:

'Was it fit that this fellow, should dare either to deride you or (which is the greater iniury) to teach you? . . . This man, whilst he lived, attributed so much to his own wit, that hee never thought himselfe beholden to your helps, and insinuations; and was so farre from invoking you, or sacrificing to you, that he did not so much as acknowledge your kingdome, nor beleeve that there was any such thing in nature, as you. I must confesse, that hee had the same opinion of God also, and therefore deserves a place here, and a better than any of the *Pagan* or *Gentile* idolaters:

[1] Gentillet C. 30–1 (Meyer cit., p. 13). Cf. *Sejanus*, III. iii: 'I have heard that aconite,/Being timely taken, hath a healing might/Against the scorpion's stroke; the proof we'll give:/That, while two poisons wrestle, we may live.'

for, in every idolatrie, and false worship, there is some Religion, and some perverse simplicitie, which tastes of humilitie; from all which, this man was very free, when in his heart he utterly denyed that there was any God. . . . But to proceed now to the iniuries, which this fellow hath done to the *Bishop* of *Rome*, although very much might be spoken, yet by this alone, his disposition may bee sufficiently discerned, that hee imputes to the *Pope*, vulgar and popular sinnes, farre unworthy of his greatnesse.   Weake praising, is a kind of Accusing, and wee detract from a mans honour, if when wee praise him for small things, and would seeme to have said all, we conceale greater.'

At this point Donne puts into the mouth of Ignatius a scurrilous attack on the sins of the popes, which covers several pages. Then Ignatius comes back to Machiavelli:

'Let us more particularly consider those things, which this man, who pretends to exceed all Auncient and Moderne *Statesmen*, boasts to have beene done by him. Though truly no man will easily beleeve, that hee hath gone farr in any thing, which did so tire at the beginning, or mid-way, that having seene the *Pope*, and knowne him, yet could never come to the knowledge of the *Divell*. . . . How idle, and how very nothings they are, which he hath shoveld together in his bookes, this makes it manifest, that some of every *Religion*, and of every profession have risen up against him and no man attempted to defend him. . . . This then is the point of which wee accuse *Machivell*, that he carried not his Mine so safely, but that the enemy perceived it still. But wee, who have received the Church to be as a ship, do freely saile in the deep sea. . . . As for that particular, wherein *Machiavel* useth especially to glory; which is, that he brought in the liberty of dissembling, and lying, it hath neither foundation nor colour: For not onely *Plato*, and other fashioners of *Commonwealths* allowed the libertie of lying, to Magistrates & to Physicians, but we also . . . have found that doctrine [in the Fathers of the Church] . . . yet wee have departed from this doctrine of free lying . . . because we were not the first *Authors* of it. But wee have supplied this losse with another doctrine, lesse suspitious; and yet of as much use to our *Church*; which is *Mentall Reservation*, and *Mixt propositions*. The libertie therefore of lying, is neither new, nor safe as almost all *Machivells* precepts are so stale and obsolete, that our *Serarius* using I must confesse his *Iesuiticall* liberty of wilde anticipation did not doubt to call *Herod*, who lived so long before *Machivell*, a *Machiavellian*.'

Loyola concludes his speech of fifty pages by saying that in all times in the Roman Church there have been friars who have far exceeded Machiavelli in his own arts. Crushed by this monumental oration, poor Machiavelli, 'often put forward, and often thrust back', at last vanishes. This truculent fight between the two Southern bugbears vies for perversity of grim humour with Richard Lovelace's account of the fight between the toad and the spider. Among the other innovators who come as claimants after Machiavelli is Pietro Aretino, but his boast of the notorious licentious pictures[1] is minimized by Ignatius's statement that the Jesuits have gone even farther, in expurgating the ancient texts not in order to destroy the obscenities, but rather in order to teach them to their disciples after having experimented 'whether *Tiberius* his *Spintria*, & *Martialis Symplegma*, and others of that kinde, were not rather *Chimeraes*, & speculations of luxuriant wits, then things certaine & constant, and such as might bee reduced to an Art and methode in licentiousnes'. Donne is surprised by the rejection of Aretino, since

'hee might have beene fit, either to serve *Ignatius*, as *maister of his pleasures*, or *Lucifer* as his *Crier*: for whatsoever Lucifer durst think, this man durst speake'.

At last Lucifer, wishing to get rid of Loyola, who threatens to become too powerful, suggests that he should withdraw with the rest of the Jesuits to the moon, and found a Lunatic Church there: 'without doubt after the Iesuites have been there a litle while, there will soone grow naturally a *Hell* in that world also'.

Also in Middleton's political play, *A Game at Chess*, we find Machiavellism and Jesuitism, this time working in agreement, in the characters of the Black Knight, i.e. the Spanish Ambassador Gondomar, and the Black Bishop's Pawn, i.e. the Jesuit Father John Floyd.[2] The Induction to this play

[1] Illustrations, after paintings by Giulio Romano, of venereal postures. Aretino was responsible for the explanatory lines.

[2] *The Works of Thomas Middleton*, ed. Bullen, vii, pp. 4 and 118.

consists in a dialogue between Ignatius Loyola, 'the great incendiary of Christendom' (II. ii. 110), and Error. Among other things Ignatius says (ll. 73–4):

> I would do any thing to rule alone:
> 'Tis rare to have the world reign'd in by one.

In this play, however, contrary to what we have seen in *Ignatius his Conclave*, the Machiavellian appears to be subtler than the Jesuit. The Black Knight says (I. i. 253 ff.):

> I have bragg'd less,
> But have done more than all the conclave on 'em,
> Take their assistant fathers in all parts,
> Yea, and their Father General in to boot.

Then follows the passage about facetious poisoning already referred to. Presently the Black Knight makes an outward show of deference towards the Black Bishop's Pawn, and says (ll. 276 ff.):

> I do this the more
> T'amaze our adversaries to behold
> The reverence we give these guitonens,
> And to beget a sound opinion
> Of holiness in them and zeal in us,
> And also to invite the like obedience
> In other pusills by our meek example.

The Black Bishop's Pawn tries to commit a rape upon the White Queen's Pawn, but when this latter accuses him to the White Queen, the Black Knight produces a pretended alibi in his defence. He would have the White Queen's Pawn for her calumny to be condemned 'in a room fill'd all of Aretine's pictures' to 'more than twice twelve labours of luxury'. One sees that in the minds of the authors of the age, Machiavelli, Loyola, and Aretino were three closely associated figures. The Black Knight is so much of a hardened politician that when his Pawn suggests that the sad news he brings may prick his conscience, he retorts (III. i. 119 ff.):

> Mine?
> Mischief must find a deep nail, and a driver
> Beyond the strength of any Machiavel
> The politic kingdoms fatten, to reach mine.

Of him says the White Duke (III. i. 202): 'I'll undertake/ 'That Knight shall teach the devil how to lie.' His soul can 'digest a monster without crudity,/A sin as weighty as an elephant/And never wamble for it' (IV. ii. 12 ff.). On hearing the White Knight call dissembling a vice, he exclaims (v. iii. 147 ff.):

> And call you that a vice?—
> Avoid all profanation, I beseech you,—
> The only prime state-virtue upon earth,
> The policy of empires
>
> .   .   .   .   .
>
> 'Tis like a jewel of that precious value
> Whose worth's not known but to the skilful lapidary.

Throughout the play the Machiavellian is represented sheltering the Jesuit and using him as a tool. Both are finally found out and confounded.

Though a touch of ridicule had been inherent from the first in the figure of the Elizabethan Machiavellian, since his tricks were bound to recoil inevitably on his own head, the loathsomeness of his character was calculated to provoke chiefly horror during the period of his greatest vogue. When the taste for poignant tragedy died down and romantic plays swayed the stage, the figure of the Machiavellian was doomed to lose its more lurid colours, in order to suit the general tuning down of passions. In an idyllic, sentimental world there was little room for Machiavelli: the audience could no longer be affected by his terrors, but became increasingly aware of his ridicule. Ridicule is only left when the tamed bugbear appears for the last time as an independent character in dramatic literature, as Lord Machavil in Aston Cokaine's *Trapolin Creduto Principe* (1657).

Though the legend of Machiavelli had been very popular in general, it had enjoyed the greatest vogue with the dramatists, first of all because it had fitted very well the stock character of the villain of Senecan extraction. As a matter of fact, it is very surprising to see how seldom popular literature of broadsides and satirical prints made use of it. *The Uncasing of Machivils Instructions to his Sonne* (1613) and *Machivells Dogge* (1617) are almost the sole instances we are able to quote in this section, and, since the latter pamphlet is an evident imitation of the former, our list is practically exhausted with one single item. In the whole catalogue of satirical prints of political and personal import relating to this period in the British Museum, the only case I have come across of allusion to Machiavelli is represented by Thomas Scott's *Vox Populi*.[1] It is natural, then, that with the closing of the theatres the Machiavellian bugbear should have faded away. But the word remained in the vocabulary and was later on freely employed in the Restoration comedy as a jocular taunt: to call a subtle woman 'a Machiavel' became quite a fad, after the example of Ben Jonson (*The Case is Altered*, IV. iv). As a scarecrow the Machiavellian had a short-lived revival with that belated Elizabethan, Nathaniel Lee. The Jesuit practically eclipsed the Machiavellian in the popular mind. The Politician of the times of James II was eminently a Jesuited Politician.

It was Romanticism which, bringing about a taste for horrors very akin to that of the Elizabethans, restored to life the old stock characters of the tyrant, the villain, and the traitor. The German Romantics were well versed in Shakespearian drama, and possibly through it they derived what Machiavellism is inherent in the characters of their fictions. Lessing was the first to revive in Germany that exotic taste for Italian passions and horrors which Walpole's *Castle of Otranto* had shortly before revived in England. The Italian background of *Emilia Galotti* is the same traditional background of the Elizabethans. Together with the poniards and the banditti—inevitable paraphernalia—

---

[1] *The Second Part of Vox Populi, or Gondomar appearing in the likenes of Matchiavell in a Spanish Parliament, wherein are discovered his treacherous and subtile Practises To the ruine as well of England, as the Netherlandes. Faithfully Translated out of the Spanish Coppie by a well-willer to England and Holland* (1620). To this tract, written by Thomas Scott, a Scotch Minister at Utrecht, Middleton was indebted for his *Game at Chess*.

reappear the characters of the despotic prince and of the Machiavellian knave, this latter in the person of the wicked courtier Marinelli. The villainous Franz Moor in Schiller's *Räuber* is admittedly a compound of Iago, Richard III, and Edmund (in *King Lear*); Präsident von Walter in *Kabale und Liebe* is Franz Moor become a prime minister of the Machiavellian type, while his secretary, Wurm, is a still fuller incarnation of the Machiavellian politician. Tieck's Andrea Cosimo, in the epistolary novel *William Lovell*, is a Machiavellian brought up to date with a study of eighteenth-century philosophers, chiefly Condillac. He is a cold, cynical dissector of souls, who takes a perverse delight in studying the rare ways in which a soul works on another. He has devised for his own gratification a sort of jocoserious lottery of souls: this gamble is his pastime.[1] This sinister figure of romantic villain was brought to perfection by Goethe in his Mephistopheles, whose name stands in our present vocabulary for many of those characteristics the Elizabethans comprehended under the description 'Machiavellian'. How much of Mephistopheles's villainy may be traced to the influence of the Machiavellian legend is difficult to say. But Machiavellism was obviously at the back of Goethe's mind in portraying that devil, as it was in sketching that miniature Mephistopheles, Clavigo's worldly-wise councillor Carlos.[2] Mephistopheles is primarily a courtier, and

[1] *William Lovell*, Book VI, Letter vii: 'Ueberlass es mir, meine Plane zu ersinnen und zu regieren. . . . Was kümmert es Dich, wenn ich mir ein seltsames Spielwerk erlese, das mir die Zeit ausfüllt und auf meine eigene Art meinen Geist beschäftigt? Wenn ich bemerke, auf welche sonderbare Art die eine Seele auf die andere wirken kann? Du hast wohl mehrere Nächte unter Karten und Würfeln hingebracht; so vergönne mir, dass ich mir aus Menschen ein Glückspiel und ernsthaft lächerliches Lotto bilde, dass ich ihre Seelen gleichsam entkörpert vor mir spielen lasse, und ihre Vernunft und ihr Gefühl wie Affen an Ketten hinter mir führe.' For Cosimo's sensationism see Letter xiii in the same Book.

[2] Clavigo's story shows some similarities with the Faust-Gretchen episode; with the difference that the girl's brother here kills the faithless lover (Beaumarchais is the counterpart of Valentin). Carlos's role

shows at his best at the Kaiser's Court, when he advocates
the famous device for restoring the finances of the State.
On hearing his words about the inborn spiritual power of
the gifted man—corresponding to Machiavelli's *virtù*—the
Chancellor accuses him of atheism. When Faust turns
conqueror, Mephistopheles turns pirate and repeats the
famous maxim of Machiavellism: 'If one has might, one
has right: one asks about *what*, and not about *how*.' That is,
the end justifies the means. But apart from his treacherous
help in killing Valentin, and from his scaring to death
Philemon and Baucis, Goethe's Mephistopheles does not
display a tenth of the ferocious perfidy of the Elizabethan
villains. The study of the *Encyclopédistes*—who, by the way,
knew their Machiavelli—has refined him thoroughly. He
is the less harmful among the demons, *der Schalk*, the rogue,
endowed with something of the attractive humour of Fal-
staff. In Mephistopheles nothing is left of the beast-like
figure of the Devil, with pointed horns, flaming eyes, and
protruding tusks: of the medieval monster only the gentle
satyr's cloven foot is kept. His malign power is all concen-
trated in the mind, and the mind has been trained at the
school of his ancient disciple become, in his turn, his master,
the legendary Machiavelli.

corresponds to Mephistopheles's. His arguments to persuade Clavigo
to jilt Marie have a true Machiavellian ring. Cf. IV. i: 'Aber auch da,
Clavigo, sei ein ganzer Kerl und mache deinen Weg stracks, ohne
rechts und links zu sehen. Möge deine Seele sich erweitern, und die
Gewissheit des grossen Gefühls über dich kommen, dass ausserordentliche Menschen eben auch darin ausserordentliche Menschen sind, weil
ihre Pflichten von den Pflichten des gemeinen Menschen abgehen; dass
der, dessen Werk es ist ein grosses Ganze zu übersehen, zu regieren, zu
erhalten, sich keinen Vorwurf zu machen braucht, geringe Verhält-
nisse vernachlässiget, Kleinigkeiten dem Wohl des Ganzen aufgeopfert
zu haben. Thut das der Schöpfer in seiner Natur, der König in seinem
Staate: warum sollten wir's nicht thun, um ihnen ähnlich zu werden?'
To Clavigo's objection, 'Carlos, ich bin ein kleiner Mensch,' he replies,
'Wir sind nicht klein, wenn Umstände uns zu schaffen machen, nur
wenn sie uns überwältigen.' On the point of death Clavigo says to him:
'Höre mich, Carlos! Du siehst hier die Opfer deiner Klugheit—.'